nickelodeon™

THE LEGEND OF KORRA™

AN AVATAR'S CHRONICLE

nickelodeon™

THE LEGEND OF KORRA™

AN AVATAR'S CHRONICLE

Text by Andrea Robinson

Original illustrations by Sora Medina

INSIGHT
EDITIONS

San Rafael, California

INTRODUCTION

To the Future Avatar This May Concern:

Now that Asami and I are back from the Spirit World, Tenzin has asked that I spend some time recording and reflecting on the events I've experienced as the Avatar since stealing away to Republic City and Air Temple Island so long ago.

In short—

I didn't know how to airbend, then I faced Amon and the Equalists and learned how to airbend. I made an itsy-bitsy mistake and trusted my uncle Unalaq, who didn't really have my best interests in mind. My uncle's actions led to the reemergence of Vaatu and a Water Tribe civil war, but I stopped that by becoming big and blue and reuniting the Spirit World with our world through a new spirit portal. That reunion created a new generation of Airbenders, who were unfortunately kidnapped by an anarchist group that wanted to destroy the Avatar Cycle forever. I gave myself up in exchange for their safety. After a few dark years that are better to skip over, I came back just in time to help stop a Metalbender named Kuvira from taking over Republic City with her Earth Empire Army and a giant mecha suit. (It was seriously giant!)

Now I am doing my best as the Avatar to help rebuild Republic City around the new spirit portal and maintain balance and peace in the world. I do all of this with the guidance of my mentor, Tenzin, who, apart from his love of unnecessary written assignments, has provided me with large amounts of wise and thoughtful counsel for which I am eternally grateful.

Really.

I've learned.

I've grown.

And now, I've recorded.

The End.

Sincerely,

Avatar Korra

While I appreciate the effusive—and not at all obsequious—praise, you need to go deeper for this assignment. I know that you are busy and that you have a lot on your plate, but we are living in a world where future Avatars may not have connections to their past lives. A record of your significant accomplishments and battles will likely be invaluable. And make no mistake, your accomplishments are significant, Korra, and impressive. Try again. It's my hope to see this book's pages filled. I want future generations, and future Avatars, to know you as I have come to know and appreciate you.

—Tenzin

I completely understand. And because of that, I have recruited leading experts on my journey as Avatar. Their authority will make this a record for the ages.

—Korra

Filled with words, Korra. Not drawings from my children.

Good place for belly rubs.

Avatar Korra, Triumphant, with Large Dog
by the artist Ikki.

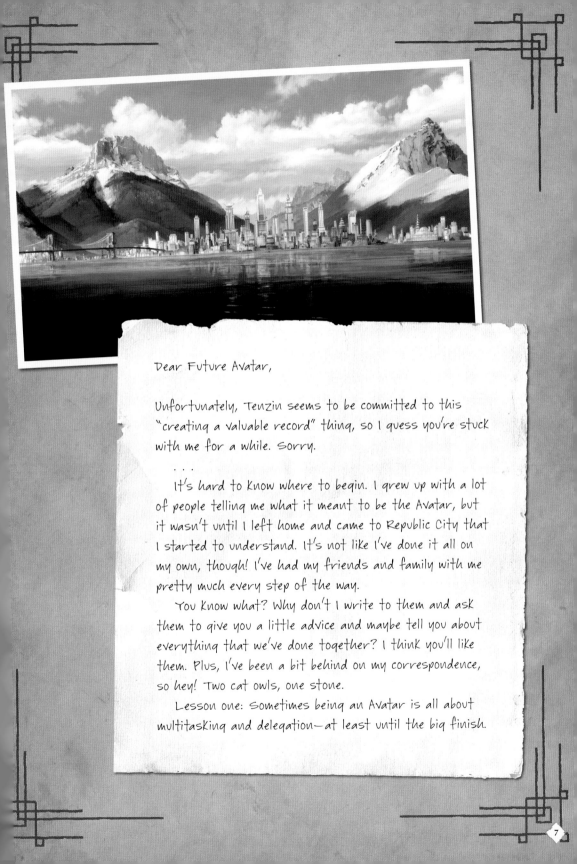

Dear Future Avatar,

Unfortunately, Tenzin seems to be committed to this "creating a valuable record" thing, so I guess you're stuck with me for a while. Sorry.

. . .

It's hard to know where to begin. I grew up with a lot of people telling me what it meant to be the Avatar, but it wasn't until I left home and came to Republic City that I started to understand. It's not like I've done it all on my own, though! I've had my friends and family with me pretty much every step of the way.

You know what? Why don't I write to them and ask them to give you a little advice and maybe tell you about everything that we've done together? I think you'll like them. Plus, I've been a bit behind on my correspondence, so hey! Two cat owls, one stone.

Lesson one: Sometimes being an Avatar is all about multitasking and delegation—at least until the big finish.

Dear Korra,

It was an unexpected blessing to receive your letter, and I'm always happy for an excuse to speak more about the history of the Water Tribes, given that our future was in jeopardy not so long ago. With my daughter Kya busy in Republic City helping with the efforts to resettle refugees, I find that I could use the company, even if it is long-distance.

Now that I am older, I can see that my childhood was defined by those who were missing—my mother after she passed and my father gone away to fight in the Hundred Year War. It was only after Sokka and I discovered Aang in the ice that I began to discover a new sense of family, one that was at first comprised of the friends we met on our journey and, eventually, one that Aang and I would create together.

Because of that, it was a special joy to see you grow up surrounded not only by the love of your mother and father—who were so proud of their daughter, the Avatar—but also by a tribe of resilient people who have survived so many challenges, often thanks to the wise leadership of men and women like your parents.

Do you remember that day outside the hut when I told you that waterbending was done with slow, calm movements, and you ended up burying me in the snow? Your mother was so worried, but I knew it was only a matter of time. You've always been one who needed to forge ahead and find her own way, whether that meant following my son Tenzin to Republic City or withdrawing to recover from all that you faced as the Avatar. But if there's any advice I can give you (or any future incarnation) it's to never forget that there's also strength in looking back at where you've been.

Please give my love to my children and grandchildren. Oh, and tell Tenzin and his brother Bumi to be nice to one another.

Katara

I do remember that day outside the hut. I had been so frustrated with my father, who at the time seemed so concerned with the *rules* of being an Avatar. When he told me that I couldn't go play with a pack of polar bear dogs, I snuck out anyway. Unfortunately, it was in the middle of a snowstorm and I got lost. However, I did find Naga.

—Korra

NAGA

Naga is my animal guide. Apparently all Avatars have them (and here's a thank-you for letting mine be something a little more compact and grounded than Aang's air bison!). Naga's my best friend, and she's been an immense help to me over the years, helping me get around, tracking me down when I've been lost, comforting me at the end of a bad day, or okay, *occasionally* threatening to bite someone's head off to extract information.

Don't let that fool you, though—while I know she can look a little intimidating, she's really a sweetheart, especially if you have a stash of treats at all times and know how to rub her belly. A lot of friends will help you on your journey as the Avatar—I hope you have one like Naga who will always have your back.

TONRAQ AND SENNA

I knew that Katara grew up without her mother, but I guess I'd never realized how small her family started out. I've been lucky to always have the support of my parents no matter what—even if I don't always recognize it as loving support at first. Now that I'm older, I'm starting to understand that all those unnecessary rules were just my parents looking out for me, protecting me from people who would want to use the Avatar for their own ends.

My parents always did their best to protect me, and sometimes that meant protecting me from the mistakes in their own pasts. My father didn't tell me that he had been exiled from the Northern Water Tribe after his impulsive actions led to an attack from dark spirits. I found out eventually, but I wish he had told me sooner. I think it would have helped me to know that no one is perfect—not my parents, not Tenzin, not even the Avatar.

THE ORDER OF THE WHITE LOTUS

The Order of the White Lotus formed many years ago as a secret society for those who wished to transcend territory affiliation and seek truth and beauty. But since the time of Avatar Aang, the order is not so secret anymore, and one of its core missions has been to protect and train the Avatar, starting with yours truly.

They'll probably be there to look after future Avatars too. I'd be lying if I didn't say that sometimes always being under their guard will feel a little . . . intense.

THE SOUTHERN COMPOUND

When I was little, an anarchist named Zaheer tried to kidnap me. He believed that no one, especially the Avatar, should have such power. After that, my father insisted that we stay in the Southern Water Tribe Compound, with its thick walls of ice and heavy metal gate. It was there that I learned from the masters how to bend water, fire, and earth. But I was also always under the watchful eyes the Order of the White Lotus.

THE HEALING HUT

There wasn't all that much to do in the Southern Compound. I spent a lot of time in the healing hut with Katara, who taught me how to use waterbending to mend wounds and broken bones. She's one of the best healers I know, and that's still where we go for things like Jinora's spirit being separated from her body and me being poisoned by . . . you know, enough about that! No one wants a record that's all dark and depressing. Let's just say that if bad things happen, the healing hut is a good place to go.

I got another letter today, from Katara's son Bumi—the son who doesn't make me do extra homework.

AIRBENDING

Korra,

It's great to hear from you! Bum-Ju is fine and chirps hello, or at least I'm pretty sure he does. And no, I haven't shaved my head to help with my new airbending skills—you can tell my little brother that the chances of that happening are about as great as him loosening up enough to go on a vacation without a detailed itinerary. Vacation Tenzin . . . Ha!

You asked how the airbending is going now that my official training with Tenzin is over. I'll tell you one thing—there are a lot fewer boring stories about Ol' Tang Xu the Amazing Fasting Monk, that's for sure. Still, I can't be too hard on Tenzin; I know I like to bust his chops, but the only reason I feel like Dad would be proud of me now is because Tenzin's never stopped trying to teach me or believing that this old dog could learn something new.

Just don't tell him that. Don't want his tattooed head to get any bigger, ya know?

—Bumi

P.S. I don't know that I have any great advice for Avatars, but did I ever tell you the story of how I saved all of you when you were being held prisoner by Unalaq at that Northern army camp? Well, it all started with my trusty flute and a dark spirit who was a bit of a music lover . . .

I am only including the start of this letter, as Bumi's story about how he rescued us goes on for four pages, and while I'm not saying that I entirely doubt his story, the bit about the dark spirits possessing the mecha suit and inadvertently helping him knock out our guards and the entire tent feels like one of Bumi's tall tales.

His letter does make me think back to the first few weeks of my own training with Tenzin on Air Temple Island, though. I was so sure that the airbending thing would click as soon as I snuck away to Republic City, especially given Tenzin's reputation as "Mr. Spiritual." Instead, only one day in and I'm getting whacked left and right by sacred air gates while Tenzin and his three airbending prodigies are hopping up and down and yelling, "Be the leaf!" and, "Dance, dance like the wind!"

According to Tenzin, the principles of airbending are simple.

1. When you meet resistance, you must be able to switch direction at a moment's notice.
2. Employ circular movements to avoid obstacles.
3. Let your mind and spirit be free, for air is the element of freedom.
4. Meditate.
5. Meditate.
6. Meditate some more.

   (. . . Believe me, if you fall asleep, you're still meditating better than I could when I first started.)

BECOME AN EXPERT AIRBENDER
IN 30 DAYS OR LESS!
WITH WORDS AND PICTURES BY MEELO

So you woke up one day with the power to airbend. Sure, there are a lot of people who will *claim* they know how to teach you to use your newfound skills—some of them are bald and also my dad—but the fact is that there's only one surefire way to become the best Airbender that you can be, and that's the Meelo Way.*

1. Look to your left! Look to your right! One of these people will not make it out of here alive, so don't get too attached. (If you are in a room alone, you'll have to find a room with someone in it for this to work.)

2. Whatever you do, remember: Be the leaf.

3. Nontraditional sources of wind are your friend. Don't let your sisters tell you otherwise.

4. Treats are not just for ring-tailed winged lemurs anymore. Reward yourself accordingly.

*Patent pending. Not responsible for injuries sustained if subject is unable to handle that much Meelo.

These are the spinning gates Tenzin used for the first part of my Airbender training. Tragically, the original gates were, um, accidentally destroyed by fire after two thousand years of being used for ~~torture~~ training, but they've been rebuilt and have come in handy with the new generation of Airbenders.

Air Temple Island also has a meditation pavilion, which Tenzin and his children use almost daily when not under attack or off on a tour of the Air Nation's historical landmarks. Time spent here encourages discipline and patience (and for *some*, it provides a solid naptime).

Men and women have separate dorms on the island, and the sentries sent by the Order of the White Lotus have homes. A shared greenhouse supplements the island's all-vegetarian diet.

(I'm not saying you should ever do this, future Avatar, but if you ever want to maybe slip out a bit to see the city, the Order of the White Lotus has been known to be easily distracted by a pro-bending match on the radio.)

Speaking of pro-bending . . .

PRO-BENDING

For all of Tenzin's meditating, it wasn't until I snuck out and joined the Fire Ferrets as their Waterbender and had to dodge my opponent's attacks that I started to understand how to move like an Airbender. Luckily, after only *minor* grumbling that it was a waste of time, Tenzin also saw what a great training tool it was.

I just realized that I don't know if pro-bending is going to exist in the future, given that our arena was partially destroyed. I really hope that it does, but if it doesn't, here's what you need to know.

Each team is comprised of three members: a Firebender, an Earthbender, and a Waterbender (or, in very specific cases, an Avatar who has agreed to do only one of the three).

The point is to gain as much territory as possible in the arena—which is divided into three zones—with the ultimate goal of driving your opponents over the edge into the water for a knockout. If you're good enough to get a knockout, you automatically win the match; if no knockout occurs, the winner of each of the three rounds is determined by which team gained the most ground or ended with the most members still standing.

Advancement into another team's zone can only happen once you've managed to drive all three opponents out of that zone. Waterbenders can't use ice and are limited to short bursts of water. Firebenders can't throw flames in a constant blast or strike faces. Earthbenders have to avoid metalbending and are limited to the earth discs in the zone in which they are presently bending.

In the event of a tie, a single element is selected, and the respective benders duke it out on a raised platform until one is knocked off. But the most important thing to know about the history of pro-bending? The Fire Ferrets would *clearly* have won that championship game if the refs hadn't been bought off.

Even though we didn't win the championship, it was through the Fire Ferrets that I met Mako and Bolin. Together, we became the first members of what would eventually be known as Team Avatar.

This makes me wonder if every former Avatar had a team. I know Aang had Sokka, Katara, Toph, and Zuko, but the others? I feel bad for them if they didn't. I don't know that I could have accomplished all that I did without mine.

PRO-BENDING CHAMPIONSHIP

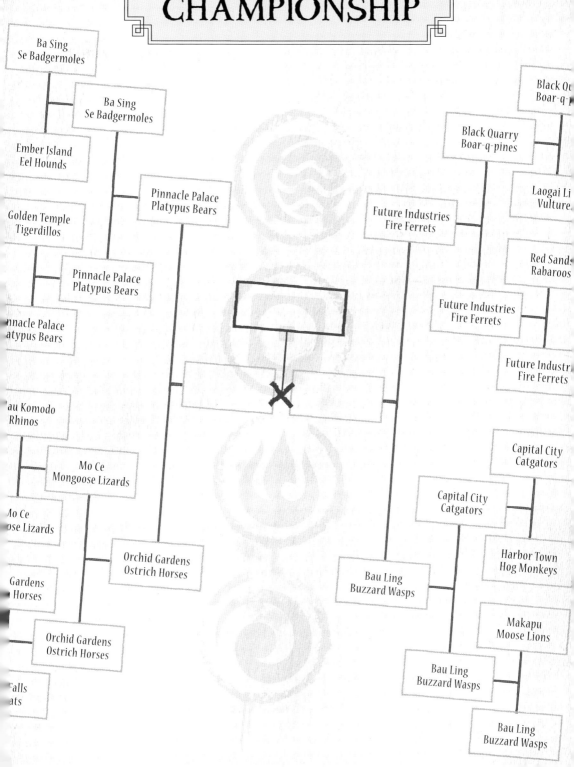

Ba Sing
Se Badgermoles

Ba Sing
Se Badgermoles

Ember Island
Eel Hounds

Pinnacle Palace
Platypus Bears

Golden Temple
Tigerdillos

Pinnacle Palace
Platypus Bears

nnacle Palace
atypus Bears

au Komodo
Rhinos

Mo Ce
Mongoose Lizards

Mo Ce
ose Lizards

Orchid Gardens
Ostrich Horses

Gardens
Horses

Orchid Gardens
Ostrich Horses

alls
ats

Black Qu
Boar-q-

Black Quarry
Boar-q-pines

Future Industries
Fire Ferrets

Laogai Li
Vulture

Red Sand
Rabaroos

Future Industries
Fire Ferrets

Future Industr
Fire Ferrets

Capital City
Catgators

Capital City
Catgators

Harbor Town
Hog Monkeys

Bau Ling
Buzzard Wasps

Makapu
Moose Lions

Bau Ling
Buzzard Wasps

Bau Ling
Buzzard Wasps

REPUBLIC CITY

MAKO'S COOL POLICE SAYINGS

E FOUR OTHER LETTERS THAT
A CHANCE TO RESPOND. I'VE BEEN
EING PART OF THE REPUBLIC CITY
DING PRINCE WU. THANKFULLY,
O UP. NOW I JUST WISH HE'D
R THE ALBUM OF BADGERMOLE

ACCOMMODATE THE NEW SPIRIT
A LOT OF UNREST WITH THE
EMPORARY PARTNER—AND I ARE
TIME AS DETECTIVES. I THINK
LIN IS EVEN STARTING TO LIKE ME . . . OR MAYBE SHE DID ALL ALONG. I
KNOW YOU'LL PROBABLY FIND THIS HARD TO BELIEVE, BUT I SOMETIMES HAVE
TROUBLE READING WOMEN.

WE DID HAVE A LOT OF ADVENTURES TOGETHER, DIDN'T WE? SINCE
BOLIN AND I ARE DEALING WITH THE TRIPLE THREATS AGAIN, I'VE BEEN
THINKING A LOT ABOUT YOU AND OUR EARLY DAYS TOGETHER. I'M STILL
SORRY FOR BEING SO RUDE THAT FIRST DAY AT THE GYM. I DON'T KNOW
WHAT I WOULD DO IF WE'D NEVER BECOME FRIENDS.

NO MATTER WHAT HAPPENS, I MEANT WHAT I SAID ABOUT ALWAYS
HAVING YOUR BACK.

SINCERELY,

MAKO

P.S. I'VE STILL BEEN WORKING ON MY LIST OF COOL POLICE SAYINGS. OKAY, SOME OF
THEM I DIDN'T THINK OF UNTIL AFTER THEY WERE USEFUL, BUT STILL . . .

Korra,

It's about time I got a letter from you! I spent some time doing a little pen pal math last night, and if my calculations are correct, Pabu and I have poured our hearts out into twenty-three letters—only ten of which were, as you put it, "grossly melodramatic"—and yet this is the first one we've received in return. I don't mind, but Pabu . . . Pabu feels things, Korra.

Life as Mako's partner on the police force—Mako's favorite, best, most talented partner—is going well, and I'm at least 99 percent sure that this job won't end with me fleeing through the forest for fear of being thrown in a reeducation camp—which, by the way, is not a place where they teach you new craft skills . . . just in case you, and you alone, were under any false impressions.

Opal's much happier with this job, too, and she likes this uniform a lot better than my old Earth Empire one (although a little bit less than my Nuktuk shorts . . . but moving on).

I really can't complain about anything in my life right now. I've got a great job, and I'm in the best and least frighteningly aggressive relationship I've ever had, even if there is quite a bit of kale.

So. Much. Kale.

~~Please save me from the kale.~~

Anyhoo, I'm still waiting for you to come visit with my new extended Earthbender family. I think a few of them are starting to doubt my claims that the Avatar and I are best friends. My cousin Big Ti still believes me, but Little Ti . . . I would hate to disappoint him.

Lots of Love,

Bolin

P.S. I'm including one of my Nuktuk mover headshots, as while I may have unfortunately melted my beautiful, beautiful statue / hat rack while showing off my lavabending to Medium Yu, I still have a million of these things. You're welcome.

Sometimes it's hard to believe how much has changed in just four years. When I first met Mako and Bolin, they were fresh from working for the Triple Threats, just barely making rent living above the pro-bending arena and not on the streets. Now they're Republic City detectives keeping those same streets safe so we never have to worry about crazy revolutionaries trying to destroy people's bending abilities, or—

Er, anyway, moving on. We're all busy, I know, but sometimes I do miss the old days, when it'd be rare for a day to go by without hearing their brotherly bickering or watching some new trick that Bolin taught Pabu.

It's crazy, really, when you think about how much Republic City has changed ever since Aang and Zuko established it so many years ago on what was once territory of the Fire Nation. Maybe that's where its strength comes from: knowing how to change. It's faced so many threats over the years, each of which left its mark, and yet somehow, it's still standing. Maybe that's why it's come to feel so much like home. Or maybe it's because so many of my friends call it home.

REPUBLIC CITY PARK

One of my favorite places in the city is Republic City Park—or Avatar Korra Park, although I have a hard time calling it that. Tenzin is always insisting that I should, saying that the renaming is a sign of the people's appreciation for what I've done and what I will—hopefully—do in the future. There's even a statue.

Still, maybe in some weird way it is appropriate that it bears my name, as it was the first place I went after hopping off the boat with Naga. Even after everything, it remains a good place to do some tai chi, pick up a game of Pai Sho, or hop up on a soapbox. (Note to self: Remember to suggest that fishing be legalized.)

CENTRAL CITY STATION

When I first came to Republic City, Central City Station was where you went to get your pockets picked. Thanks to the *brilliant* new CEO of Future Industries, though, it was revamped recently to better connect the city with the Earth Kingdom. Granted, the tunnels were a bit demolished when a large part of the populace was—temporarily!—forced to flee, but I have no doubt they will be back up and running soon.

SPIRIT WILDS

The Spirit Wilds popped up recently in Republic City, and while there were a couple of minor hiccups—just little things like the complete and total destruction of good friends' apartments and tourists' souls being kidnapped and held in the Spirit World—I'd say that they've settled down and become a unique part of the urban landscape, especially with the minds at Future Industries working on the infrastructure front. Have I mentioned that the new leader of Future Industries is pretty great?

TECHNOLOGY

Dear Korra,

I have to admit, I was a little bit surprised to receive your letter the other day, given that many of these questions about Future Industries could easily be asked in person . . . say, over a nice, romantic dinner at Fan's Dumplings? Hmmm—this wouldn't have anything to do with that assignment Tenzin gave you, would it?

Still, I'm always happy to write back. It reminds me of old times, back when you were recovering with Katara in the South, I was here in Republic City, and all that connected us were the letters we wrote each other. Even though I knew you were struggling, and even when I wasn't sure what I felt about Future Industries, just seeing your handwriting appear on my desk could brighten my whole day.

For such a long time, I felt like it was my duty to keep the family business going, for the sake of the city and the people it employed. But ever since I made peace with my father, it's become important to me that I protect his legacy. While I know that he made many mistakes, he made the ultimate sacrifice to correct those mistakes, and he helped protect us all in the end. I want that to count for something.

I know if he were here he would be doing everything he could to help rebuild the city—to create better housing developments and refine our technology to help effect the change you've spoken about so eloquently. So that's what I intend to do as well. And if the technology can help you as the Avatar—and future Avatars—then that makes me even happier.

Below are drawings and diagrams that show how Future Industries' machines and technology have already evolved over a few short years. If we do our job right, they'll soon evolve even more, helping benders and nonbenders alike. Perhaps a future Avatar will look back at these sketches and marvel at how far we've come.

I hope this is helpful for your book—if not, let me know tonight, I'm looking forward to seeing you.

Love,

Asami

ELECTRIFIED GLOVE

While it's true that my father developed this to help Amon's Equalists in their misguided attempts to rid the world of bending, I can't deny that it's been a helpful piece of equipment for a nonbender who has a tendency to pal around with the Avatar! Primarily made of metal, the gloves have a circular pad on the palm that helps the wearer give an electrified punch. They can be worn on two hands, but one tends to do the trick.

I can vouch for this.
—Korra

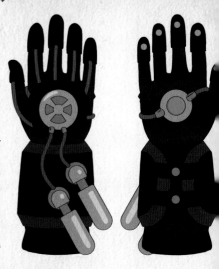

WINGSUIT

The wingsuit is one of my own inventions, designe to accommodate the growing demand for Airbende accessories after the Harmonic Convergence. Some traditionalists will always prefer to use an Airbender staff—ahem—but the sleekness of the suit does give an aerodynamic boost and provide more maneuverability, all while minimizing wind resistance. Not to mention that the color schem is a favorite of mine.

MECHA TANK

Another invention of my father's during his time working with the Equalists, this was an early prototype for the mecha suits that were quickly assimilated into many of our world's competing armies. Sometimes, I find it hard to believe that the basic concept is actually quite similar to a Future Industries forklift. He designed them to be platinum so that they could resist the Metalbenders of Republic City's police force.

FUTURE INDUSTRIES AIRSHIPS

I've seen the airships our competitors make, and I'm happy to say that none parallel my father's in quality, practical application, or sheer luxury. Extra points for the high-ceilinged gallery and the outside deck that (as we discovered on our trip to the Earth Kingdom to round up new Airbenders), has plenty of room for bending practice.

SATOMOBILE

Future Industries wouldn't be where it is today without the Satomobile, which my father first imagined when he was just a poor shoe shiner thinking of ways to make life better for the common man. While we've added new customization options and models over the years—as well as mopeds, roadsters, and even racecars—it's important to me that it never become out of reach for the average Republic City citizen. We're already busy developing the next generation of the Satomobile. I can't wait for it to hit the streets.

Hey kid,

As requested, included are the suit blueprints you wanted. Although, for the record, you should know that ever since I got this whole "conscience" thing, Varrick Industries has been shying away from any projects that could <u>allegedly</u> be turned into a linchpin for tyrannical plots of world domination.

   Instead, while Zhu Li is delving into the wide world of politics, I've turned my mind to percolating on an exciting new market: products for the happily married man! Sure, Zhu Li didn't really like the prototype for the Endearment Generator—I still say we should get a focus group going on "my winsome wolfbat"—but a new business venture will always have a few kinks to work out.

   I gotta sign off, as it's going on four o'clock and I've only got five minutes of daily productivity left. Also, if I've learned it once, I've learned it a thousand times—writing while hanging upside down quickly leads to fainting.

In wedded bliss,

Varrick

P.S. Zhu Li, my winsome wo—er, wife, when you're reading this over to catch errors and "unnecessary self-aggrandizement," please make sure to do the thing.

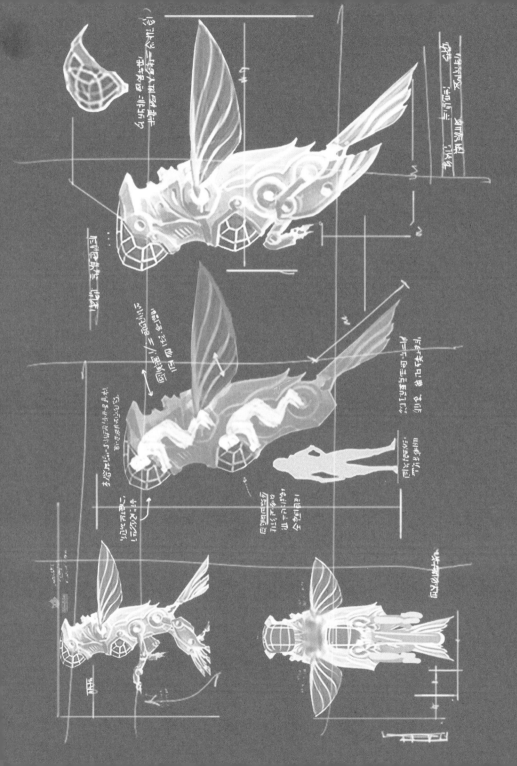

See what I mean about brilliant?

I'm constantly amazed by what Asami creates, even though every time I feel like I've got a handle on how to drive something more technologically advanced than a polar bear dog, she (or Varrick) are already cooking up the next new thing.

Maybe this won't be a struggle for you, future Avatar, but here's something that your mentor may not tell you: People will surprise you. Just when you think you can write someone off, *boom*! That's when they'll decide to show you their best. It happened with Asami's father. It happened with Varrick. The trick is trusting that everyone has reasons for their actions.

I guess what I'm trying to say is that sometimes it will be just as difficult to understand the human world as it will be to understand the Spirit World. And if you're anything like me, it may be difficult to just *get* to the Spirit World. Luckily, I had a good teacher.

SPIRITBENDING AND THE SPIRIT WORLD

Pema's Coconut Macaroons

6 cups unsweetened coconut flakes
1 tablespoon melted coconut oil
2 tablespoons maple syrup
½ teaspoon vanilla

Directions:

1. Preheat oven to 325°F.

2. Mix together the coconut flakes, coconut oil, maple syrup, and vanilla in a large bowl that is as unbreakable and air current resistant as possible.

3. Form the mixture into 1-inch mounds, and bake for 25-30 minutes at 325°F until the tops are golden, or longer if you hear a crash coming from another room and need to go investigate.

4. Most importantly—keep Meelo out of the kitchen for all of this.

Love,
Your mother

his huge Spirit Library and how I'd update its section on modern technology. Wan Shi Tong's Knowledge Seeker fox spirits seem to have some very select blind spots.

I haven't been able to explore as much as I'd like, what with all the goings-on in Republic City right now, but I still hope to take Kai—or as my dad likes to call him, "that close friend of Jinora's who is also a boy"—to the Spirit World. Kai's always been so encouraging of my airbending, and he's been right with me as we work to defend the new spirit portal in Republic City.

You asked if I could explain how I use my spirit energy to find people, but it's hard to put into exact words. All I can say is that it's like airbending, with a little spiritual stuff thrown in. Kind of a vague recipe, I know—let me know if you want the one for my mother's coconut macaroons. It's a little easier to follow.

Love,
Jinora

When I was born, the spirit portals were closed, and had been for thousands of years. The only way to enter the Spirit World was to go to the North or South Pole or to be so in tune with the spiritual plane that your spirit could journey to one of the poles on its own.

As I've probably established by now, I've always had more of a connection to the physical aspects of being the Avatar than the spiritual ones. Given that connecting with the spiritual plane takes focus and calm and many minutes of sitting in one place and . . . well, you get the picture.

The only reason I made it to the Spirit World the first time was because of Jinora, Tenzin's eldest daughter, who has always had a special connection to the spiritual side. Seeing the way she loves and respects it has helped me learn to do the same.

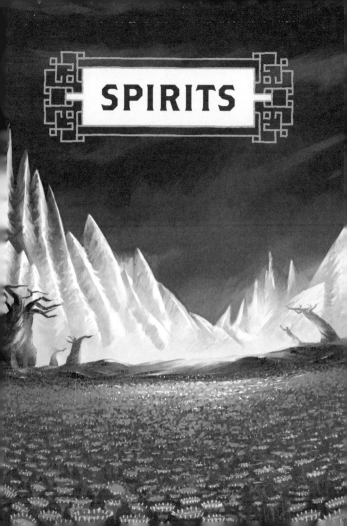

SPIRITS

Spirits exist in many forms, often appearing in plant or animallike shapes. But some can be transformed.

DARK SPIRITS

No matter how frightening they may at first appear, dark spirits are not evil. Instead, they are spirits that have become so unbalanced that they are no longer able to respond to the light within them. Even before the spirit portals were permanently open, dark spirits would sometimes appear in the physical world when sacred spots were threatened or left neglected for too long.

As an Avatar, you can help change a dark spirit's energy to positive energy through a practice called spiritbending, where you surround a spirit in healing water until it becomes calm and glows with a golden light.

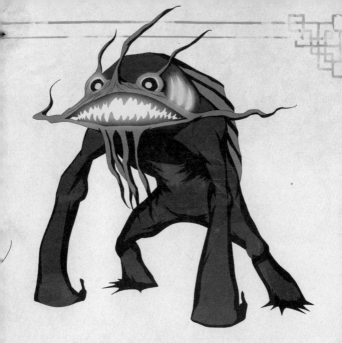

But as with any bending art, spiritbending can be abused—turning a light spirit dark or even snuffing out a human soul. Then there are times when a spirit's darkness is too great and you end up being dragged out of the ocean with temporary amnesia and no connection to your past lives (again . . . that's just been my experience).

There was an upside, though. While I was recovering after battling that dark spirit in the Mo Ce Sea, I was able to learn the story of the first Avatar, Wan.

SPIRITUAL PROJECTION

One of Jinora's many talents is spiritual projection, a special kind of energybending through which her spirit travels to distant locations in a matter of minutes while her body remains behind in the physical world. She's used it more than once to get me out of a tight spot, zeroing in on spiritual energy to find where I'm being held, eavesdrop in on important information, or even assist in a battle. Maybe you'll be able to do this too!

DRAGONFLY BUNNY SPIRITS

We discovered Jinora's talents at the Eastern Air Temple after Jinora revealed that her "invisible friends" were really dragonfly bunny spirits. Bunny spirits don't appear unless they feel a strong spiritual connection with someone, and so while some of us remain bunnyless, Jinora was able to adopt one she named Furry-Foot, and Bumi one he calls Bum-Ju—short for, you guessed it, Bumi Jr.

DRAGON BIRD SPIRITS

Although they may startle unsuspecting Avatars, dragon bird spirits are beautiful and provide a good way of getting around the Spirit World—or making a quick exit from battle. They nest on the top of Hai-Riyo Peak.

Dear Avatar Korra,

Thank you for your letter. This may surprise you, but I have been following your return to the world with interest. I think often of our last conversation, standing beside my dragon Druk at the Misty Palms Oasis. Aang would be proud of you for doing everything in your power to ensure that the Air Nation would flourish.

You mentioned that you met with my uncle Iroh in the Spirit World, and he advised you to speak with me. I admit my first impulse was to be jealous that you had seen him; I often wish that I could sit down with him now and listen to what he has to say. I know that without his guidance I would never have found my rightful purpose. If you ever happen to see him again, please let me know what you discuss. I can only hope that it will be over a good pot of rare white dragon bush tea and a challenging game of Pai Sho.

It gives me great pride that Iroh believed me worthy to counsel you, but I think it's best to pass on words from Iroh himself: While it's always best to believe in oneself, a little help from others can be a great blessing.

Sincerely,

Lord Zuko

I learned firsthand how good Lord Zuko's uncle Iroh was at giving advice. After all, he taught me the most important rule of traveling in the Spirit World: If you look for the light, you'll find the light, but if you let yourself be overwhelmed by the dark, you may be attacked by meerkats and regress into a four-year-old. (Well . . . at least that's what happened to me.)

The Spirit World is influenced by the will of those who enter it. As the bridge between the spiritual and physical planes, Avatars have even more power to change the energy of the Spirit World landscape and the spirits that inhabit it.

You, future Avatar, have the power to make it a beautiful place, with fields of flowers and mountains with nesting dragon birds . . . or you can make it a spooky forest full of dark, angry spirits. It's truly up to you (scary, I know).

THE FIRST AVATAR

Wan lived ten thousand years ago, when the only human cities in the Spirit Wilds lived on the backs of ancient Lion Turtles. Poor but sharp-witted, Wan survived in a simple tree house by stealing food, often from the stashes of the wealthy Chou family, and resented them for the sway their money had over the lives of the city's inhabitants.

One day, Wan joined a group of hunters who petitioned the city's Lion Turtle for firebending ability so they could procure food. After being granted the power, however, Wan returned to the city, where he used his new bending powers to take on the Chou family.

He failed and was banished into the Spirit Wilds forever with only his stolen firebending to protect him.

Wan's first few days mingling with the spirits went about as well as mine—think bees, carnivorous plants, complete and total rejection—but after he impressed an aye-aye spirit with his selflessness in saving a cat deer, he was accepted in the Spirit Oasis as one of the spirits' own.

But Wan hungered for more and set out to find other Lion Turtle cities. His journey was interrupted when he came upon a field where two large spirits—one light, one dark—were tangled in a fierce battle that was causing panic in the surrounding landscape.

The dark spirit pleaded with Wan to intervene, saying that the light spirit had tormented him for ten thousand years. It wasn't until Wan used his firebending to separate the two spirits that the light spirit told him the truth.

She was Raava, the spirit of peace and light, and the other was Vaatu, the spirit of darkness and chaos. By freeing Vaatu, Wan had invited chaos into the world.

Wanting to rectify his mistake, Wan devoted himself to helping Raava, petitioning the other Lion Turtles for their gifts of airbending, waterbending, and earthbending. Raava, impressed by Wan's courage and selflessness in the face of steep odds, merged with Wan, giving him the power to bend all four elements at once, thereby making him the first Avatar. With this, Wan imprisoned Vaatu in the Tree of Time for the next ten thousand years.

Wan decided the best way to maintain peace was to separate the human and spirit worlds, and so he closed the spirit portals and became the only link between the two.

Even with Vaatu locked away, Wan could never stop darkness from growing in the hearts of men. When Wan died on the battlefield, Raava promised him that the fight was not over and that she would continue to promote harmony with him through many future lifetimes. Thus, the Avatar Cycle had begun. It's this connection to the spirit Raava that gives Avatars our power and our purpose.

The spirit portals remained closed until the next Harmonic Convergence ten thousand years later—which just happened to be during my lifetime—when it was time for the forces of light to battle the forces of darkness once again.

ZAOFU AND TOPH

Dear Avatar,

Thank you for your letter, although it seems Detective Mako [remembers?]
his tenure on my force very differently. I remember him b[reaking up?]
twelve-toed gangsters, loudly breaking up with his volatil[e...]
inciting the Republic City populace over the radio with [...]

I suppose he has improved, and I have to admit tha[t...]
be good. I do consider him a valuable part of my team. A[nd I've told him?]
to stay away from the Varri-cakes at public functions, whic[h...]
in my employ (like his brother Bolin).

You ask if I've been in touch with my sister, Su. Yes, I am happy to s[ay the]
understanding we found while attempting to protect you from the Red Lotus and defend the
city against Kuvira's army has held. I've visited my nieces and nephews and that ridiculous chef
of Su's several times.

I would hope that any new Avatar would have the skills to figure out what being an Avatar
means for him or herself. But perhaps you should tell them to make sure to learn the rules
before barging in somewhere. I assume he or she, at least, wouldn't want to waste the local
police force's time.

Sincerely,
Chief Beifong

I'd like to claim that she's talking about a different "volatile" Avatar here, but as you've probably
gathered by now, there's only one Avatar per generation. I may have used my bending to throw
around a few small office items. Like a desk. It's true that our first meeting was a little rocky, but
here's a good tip—make friends with the local police *before* you decide to step in and help take
down any local gang members. Otherwise you might get arrested for disturbing the police.

Still, although Beifong is a stickler for the rules, you won't find anyone more trustworthy or
true when it comes to defending what is right. She even sacrificed her earthbending ability to
protect Tenzin and his family from Amon. I was able to give it back—all Avatars have the ability
to manipulate chi to take away or restore bending abilities once we've unlocked our Avatar
State—but she didn't know that when she put her abilities on the line.

Remember what I said about people surprising you? Beifong may seem tough as nails, but
when you need someone you can count on, she's pure gold.

Dear Korra,

Bolin told me that I'd probably be receiving a letter from you soon! I was very happy to find out he was more right about this than he was about the kale shortage he keeps insisting is coming . . .

You asked if I could share a little bit about what it was like growing up in Zaofu. My mother always told me that she designed the city to be a center of innovation and progress, but for a long time, I don't think I ever really saw it, even though I knew I should admire its state-of-the-art rail system, its beautiful metallic domes, and its culture of truth and truth-tellers.

It wasn't until you and Bolin and Aunt Lin and all the others arrived to take me away for Airbender training that I was able to find that perspective.

I can't believe that you're asking me to give advice to an Avatar, but if I had to, I guess it would be that sometimes you need a little distance to be able to see things clearly. Zaofu isn't perfect—no city can ever be totally safe, no matter how high the walls—but leaving for a while let me see that it is beautiful. I will always hold a space for it in my heart. I know that the beautiful metal domes are gone now, torn down to make Kuvira's weapon, but they will always gleam in my imagination. So will the statues of my grandmother Toph, who should be proud of the metalbending city her daughter founded.

Sincerely,

Opal

What can I say about Toph Beifong? She's a crankier, sterner, tougher-love version of Lin. I know—hard to believe, right? But I can't deny that I owe her for getting me back on my feet after some pretty tough times.

I had been wandering for a while, cut off from a lot of my friends, when she found me passed out in a puddle of mud in the middle of Foggy Swamp. She dragged me back to her home in an old tree, fed me some weird soup, and then told me that she was going to train me because she "couldn't stand to see me getting my butt kicked all the time."

Not going to lie, being told I was the worst of the two Avatars she had trained stung. I mean, she'd only trained *two*, one of whom had ended a war that had gone on for *a hundred years*. We can all admit that's a really high bar, right? *Right?*

Anyway, after more of Toph's soul-kicking, she convinced me the emotional and mental battles that were tripping me up were all in the past and that, in order to move forward, all I needed to do was let go of the fear connected to them.

So I did. And she was right. I came back.

So that's it, future Avatar. If your time as Avatar goes anything like mine, you'll learn to bend some stuff, fight some stuff, change some stuff, pull yourself out of a mud puddle, hopefully maintain balance the best you can, and maybe even save the world a few times.

Really.

I've learned a lot along the way. (I've learned so many things that, hey! Would you look at that? This book is almost full.)

I've grown. (Just like the length of this book has grown thanks to the letters from my wise and experienced friends!)

And now I've recorded. (Wouldn't you say that I've recorded, Tenzin?)

Korra, while I am willing to concede that your decision to step outside the bounds of the original assignment has in fact yielded an impressive level of detail that could be useful for understanding the times we are living in, I do believe that there is an important piece of your story missing. As unpleasant as it can be to think over times of suffering, it can be helpful to discuss the forces that you've battled—Amon and the Equalists, Unalaq, Zaheer and the Red Lotus, even Kuvira—and tell us what you've learned. Where you failed. How you triumphed.

—Tenzin

Did you skip the section where I talked about Toph? You read what she said. Past battles are in the past—I have to let go of them. What's to be gained by dredging it all back up? You yourself said that I was finally full of hope again.

—Korra

While I admit I was not there, I believe what she said was that you should let go of your fear, not that there's nothing to learn from those struggles, those fights, those dark times. If it truly becomes too much, I won't force you, but please just try. I think you'll be surprised what you reveal.

—Tenzin

Okay . . . fine. But if I disappear for another two years, this one's on you, buddy.

—Korra

ENEMIES

The truth is that sometimes I go back and read the letters from those two years away from my friends, and somehow, I still don't really know how to explain what happened. We had all been through so much, and yet for the first time, it felt like I was the only one left holding on to the pain—not only from being kidnapped by Zaheer and the Red Lotus, but also from all of the foes I had faced.

Toph once said that my enemies only did what they did because they had let themselves become unbalanced. Yet sometimes, it felt like their defeat only left an even greater imbalance to correct.

Dear Korra,
I miss you. It's not the same in Republic City without you. How are you feeling? Things are going well here. I just got a big contract to help redesign the city's infrastructure, so I'll be keeping pretty busy for a while . . .
    Still, I'm alwa~

HEY KORRA,
So, I'm NOT VERY GOOD AT WRITING LETTERS. IT'S 2:15 IN THE AFTERNOON. WEATHER IS FAIR. CHANCE OF SNOW SHOWERS LATER TODAY. BUT ENOUGH JOKING AROUND. I HOPE YOU'RE DOING WELL. ME? I'M BACK ON THE BEAT. BEIFONG HAS BEEN STAKING OUT THE RED MONSOON HIDEOUT. YOU WON'T BELIEVE WHAT'S GOING DOWN . . .

My dearest, most talented, ever-dutiful Avatar Korra,

Though several fortnights have passed since your departure to convalesce in the homeland of your tribesman, I feel our friendship knows neither time nor distance. You will be most pleased to learn that I have found gainful employment with Sir Varrick and the Lady Kuvira. I set off on the morrow with some trepidation, but I am eager to offer any aid I can in stabilizing the Earth Kingdom!

AMON AND THE EQUALISTS

Amon was the leader of the Equalists, an aggressive political faction that sprang up in Republic City in opposition to the "oppressive" actions of benders. He found a lot of support from nonbenders who feared our powers and convinced them that the spirits had given him the power to remove a person's bending ability forever—just like the Avatar.

What his followers didn't realize was that Amon was only after one thing: power. In reality, he came from a powerful Waterbender family who all had a talent for the forbidden practice of bloodbending, which allows the bender to manipulate and sometimes kill another by controlling the water in the victim's body. It used to be believed that Bloodbenders could only do this during the full moon, but Amon's father Yakone proved that a truly powerful Waterbender could bloodbend at will.

Yakone used his talents to threaten and control as one of Republic City's most notorious crime lords, until Aang took away his bending talents forever. He later escaped thanks to the help of his gang, but he passed his desire for vengeance on to his two sons, Tarrlok and Noatak.

Tarrlok hid his past and became a member of the United Republic Council, but Noatak reinvented himself as Amon to change the world as we know it. He worked with talented chi blockers (nonbenders who can temporarily shut down your bending ability using strategic, energy-interrupting hits). These chi blockers captured benders so Amon could steal their bending in very public displays of power. Amon also outfitted his soldiers with the electric gloves designed by Asami's father, Hiroshi Sato, who had been providing the rebellion with technology because of his own grief over losing his wife to bender violence.

I wish I could say that I defeated Amon easily, but he managed to defeat me and steal my bending. I unlocked my airbending in the next fight, but for a brief moment in time, I was sure that I had lost everything else forever. What's an Avatar without control over all four elements?

That was the first time that I had ever felt truly powerless. And yet, as Aang would appear to me and say, "When we hit our lowest point, we are open to the greatest change." I realized that I could unlock the Avatar State. It restored my bending and allowed me to restore the bending of all those who had lost their powers to the Equalists.

If there's any lesson to take from this, perhaps it's that it's impossible to understand the power of being the Avatar until you lose it.

Unalaq was my uncle, a powerful Waterbender and Spiritbender and the leader of the Northern Water Tribe. When I discovered that Tenzin had been a part of the decision to keep me secluded for so much of my childhood, I made the snap decision to take Unalaq for my mentor, eager to add spiritbending to my new skills as a fully realized Avatar. Unalaq seemed like the only one who knew how to control the dark spirits and turn them light again.

But my uncle was driven by ambition and thirst for power. He manipulated me into opening the Southern spirit portal, then tried to take over the Southern Water Tribe, igniting a civil war that quickly spun out of my control.

Forced to open the Northern portal to save Jinora, I wasn't able to stop Unalaq from achieving his true goal of merging with Vaatu, the dark spirit who had been imprisoned in the Tree of Time since Wan had merged with Raava, the light spirit, and defeated him ten thousand years ago. Unalaq had been plotting all along to use this new Harmonic Convergence to free Vaatu and become the Dark Avatar named Unavaatu.

As Unavaatu, the Dark Avatar separated me from Raava and severed my link with the past Avatars forever, which is why I must write this all down for you today. While I know that we can't let our failures define us, I am sorry that you won't have the connection with me, with Aang, and with all the lives that you've lived before.

I can never replace that, but luckily, with help from Jinora, I was able to stop Unavaatu—for just as light can never be truly free of darkness, darkness can never be truly free of the light. With Jinora's help, I was able to find Raava's light within the Dark Avatar, and I used that spiritbending to purify Unavaatu and stop him from letting chaos take over the world. My uncle was lost forever, but balance was restored.

Much like Wan, I made a lot of mistakes during that year, mistakes that led to a lot of suffering. But also like Wan, I did my best to learn from those and correct them, which is all any of us—Avatars included—can ever do.

ZAHEER AND THE RED LOTUS

Zaheer was an anarchist whose dream was to create a society devoid of kingdoms and spiritual leaders like the Avatar.

When his plan to kidnap me as a child was thwarted, he and his three conspirators—P'Li, Ghazan, and Ming-Hua—were imprisoned at the four corners of the world . . . which was all well and good until a certain Avatar decided to leave the spirit portals open after her battle with Unavaatu, resulting in some unexpected side effects. Suddenly, a wave of people discovered they had airbending skills. Good, right? Unfortunately, one of them was a crazed anarchist who suddenly had the power to blast out of his prison cell and jailbreak his formidable team.

P'Li was a Combustionbender, or a Firebender with the power to channel chi through her forehead and form blasts that explode on impact.

Ghazan, a Lavabender, possessed the rare ability to turn solid earth to molten rock and shoot projectiles with ease. (Of course, we have a Lavabender on Team Avatar, too, in Bolin—not that we knew that at first!)

There was also a master Waterbender, Ming-Hua, who replaced her missing arms with water and ice. She was extremely deadly.

Although my friends did their best to protect me, eventually I had a choice: Give myself up or let the growing Air Nation be destroyed before it had a chance to flourish. I chose to give myself up to Zaheer, who poisoned me with metal. He thought the pain would send me into the Avatar State, where he knew he could both destroy me and, worse, end the Avatar Cycle entirely.

I survived the poison, but it changed me. I spent years trying to find the person that I used to be. It wasn't until I found the courage to visit Zaheer in his new prison that I came to understand that it's okay to let our experiences change us. I may never be the same Korra as I was before, but this Korra can be strong in different ways.

Although I know that I've left you with a disadvantage, as the Avatar, trust that you will find different ways to be strong as well.

KUVIRA

When Zaheer assassinated Empress Hou-Ting of the Earth Kingdom, he hoped it would usher in a new era free of old power structures. Instead, he only paved the way for the rise of Kuvira, who would become one of the worst dictators the four nations had ever seen.

Kuvira was a master Metalbender who was chosen to be the Earth Kingdom's leader after the death of the Empress. At first she was hailed as the Great Uniter, offering stability and order, but in reality, she never planned to bow to royal rule; she herself meant to rule with an iron first. Instead of turning over the kingdom to Prince Wu, the rightful royal heir, Kuvira seized control of Zaofu and forged ahead with plans to expand the Earth Kingdom and claim Republic City as her own. To do this, she used Varrick's technology to create a giant spirit cannon, harvesting the spirit vines that had emerged after the Harmonic Convergence to power her weapon.

The weapon, attached to a giant mecha suit, caused massive destruction to Republic City before being brought down by Asami's and Varrick's hummingbird suits. (Luckily Varrick realized that he was on the wrong team! Remember what I said about people surprising you?)

I wanted Kuvira to surrender and see the error of her ways, but she refused to back down, and the last blast of the spirit cannon ripped open a new portal into the spirit world—but I managed to save her.

Seeing her anger at being so defeated made me think of my own failures. I realized that she and I were a lot alike, wanting to lash out at anything that made us feel vulnerable.

No matter how much power a person has, there will always be things that can make you feel vulnerable. True strength comes from recognizing that and being able to treat others who are struggling with compassion.

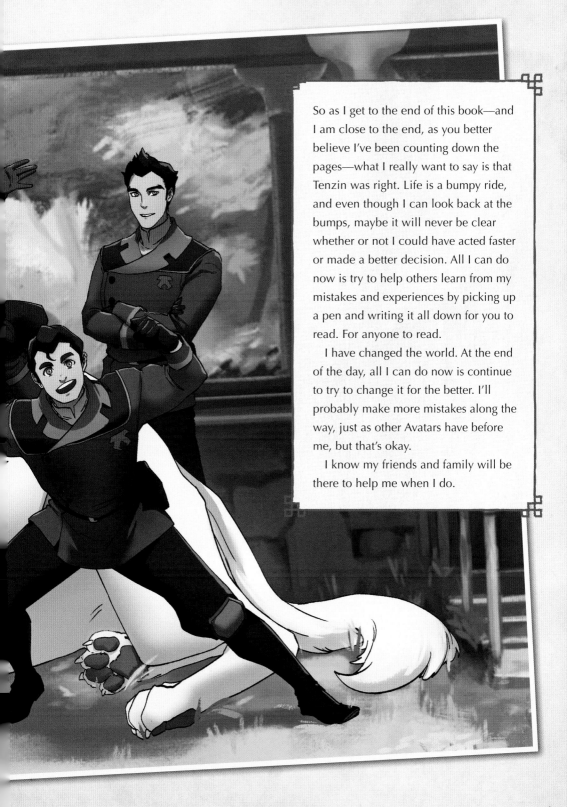

So as I get to the end of this book—and I am close to the end, as you better believe I've been counting down the pages—what I really want to say is that Tenzin was right. Life is a bumpy ride, and even though I can look back at the bumps, maybe it will never be clear whether or not I could have acted faster or made a better decision. All I can do now is try to help others learn from my mistakes and experiences by picking up a pen and writing it all down for you to read. For anyone to read.

I have changed the world. At the end of the day, all I can do now is continue to try to change it for the better. I'll probably make more mistakes along the way, just as other Avatars have before me, but that's okay.

I know my friends and family will be there to help me when I do.

INSIGHT
EDITIONS

PO Box 3088
San Rafael, CA 94912
www.insighteditions.com

Find us on Facebook: www.facebook.com/InsightEditions
Follow us on Twitter: @insighteditions

Library of Congress Cataloging-in-Publication Data available.

ISBN: 978-1-68383-393-2

Publisher: Raoul Goff
Associate Publisher: Vanessa Lopez
Creative Director: Chrissy Kwasnik
Designer: Evelyn Furuta
Senior Editor: Amanda Ng
Editorial Assistant: Maya Alpert
Senior Production Editor: Rachel Anderson
Production Manager: Sadie Crofts

ROOTS of PEACE   REPLANTED PAPER

Insight Editions, in association with Roots of Peace, will plant
two trees for each tree used in the manufacturing of this book.
Roots of Peace is an internationally renowned humanitarian
organization dedicated to eradicating land mines worldwide
and converting war-torn lands into productive farms and
wildlife habitats. Roots of Peace will plant two million fruit
and nut trees in Afghanistan and provide farmers there with
the skills and support necessary for sustainable land use.

Manufactured in China by Insight Editions

10 9 8 7 6 5 4